SUCCESSFUL RIDING

Lesley Eccles

Illustrations by Alan Batley

In association with Your Horse Magazine

First published in 1990
by Sackville Books Ltd
Stradbroke, Suffolk, England

© Sackville Books Ltd
Text © Lesley Eccles

Designed and produced by Sackville Design Group Ltd
Art Director: Rolando Ugolini
Editor: Heather Thomas

British Library Cataloguing in Publication Data
Eccles, Lesley
    Successful riding. – (Sackville Sports clinic series; 6)
    1. Livestock: Horses. Riding
    I. Title
    798.23

    ISBN 0-948615-33-8

Typeset by Hourds Typographica, Stafford

Printed and bound in Belgium by Proost Internationale
Book produktie NV, Turnhout

Contents

Lesley Eccles is the Editor of *Your Horse Magazine,* Britain's leading horse care monthly. She was formerly editor of *Horse & Pony Magazine,* the market leader for children and young riders, where she spearheaded three campaigns on equine welfare which raised in excess of £100,000 for horse charities.

A qualified journalist, Lesley worked on a large provincial newspaper before moving to public relations and then magazine journalism.

She has her own horse, which she backed and trained herself. They have competed together in long-distance riding, dressage, show-jumping, cross-country and one-day events and, Lesley's favourite pastime, drag-hunting.

She has written eight books on horses and riding and has contributed to many equestrian publications and magazines.

Introduction

Riders come in many varieties: there are those whose riding consists of a weekly lesson at the local school; others who are fairweather riders, simply hacking out in summer; some who are owners and yet have no further ambitions than to ride around the countryside safely; others, who may not necessarily be horse owners but who sincerely want to progress with their chosen sport.

All these people will benefit from an improved understanding of their mounts, and just as we have many different types of rider so we have horses who are also individuals. This point is extremely relevant for only by appreciating that an individual horse needs riding and caring for, in the most suitable way for him, can a rider hope to achieve any small measure of success.

Although there are certain ground rules for riding there also has to be flexibility – what works for one combination of horse and rider may not work for another. Get a group of riders together and they will have numerous different approaches to the same problem, derived from their personal experiences.

There is no one method or answer that makes someone a successful rider. A large number of variables are involved. If you keep an open mind, try to continually improve your knowledge and understanding of your sport, and be flexible, then you will be on the right path.

Note: I have referred to the rider throughout as 'she', and to the horse as 'he'. However, the book is equally relevant, of course, to male riders.

CHAPTER ONE

Horse and rider psychology

In most sports, success is achieved through a combination of factors. Among them are an individual's talent, training opportunities, dedication, advice from experts and sheer persistence in the face of adversity.

Horse riders require all these attributes plus the ability to forge a special relationship with their partner in sport, the horse. As well as developing their own potential, riders have to systematically train their horses so, as sportspeople, their task is double that of golfers or athletes, for example.

The horse's viewpoint

Horses are not machines. They are living creatures who, like humans, have fears, suffer confidence crises and have their own individual talents and limitations. They have 'off' days just as we do, they can suffer from insecurity, and, like

Money cannot buy success with horses. Only time and a willingness on the part of the rider to build up a relationship with the horse will bring results. A good competition horse may give a poor rider some initial success but long term, the partnership is likely to fail.

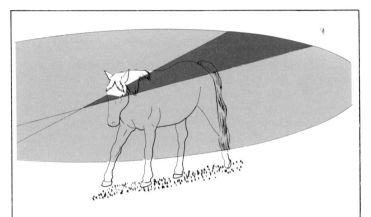

The range of a horse's eyesight: he cannot see directly behind him or immediately in front of him. Always speak to a horse to let him know you are approaching. Horses who know your voice are unlikely to move away from you even if you walk straight up to them. If the horse does not know you, he may step backwards so that he can see you, or he may turn his head, again so that he can keep you in his vision. Newcomers to horses can interpret this behaviour as unfriendliness on the horse's part or, in the case of a horse being approached in the field, as an unwillingness to be caught. Yet all the horse is doing is trying to see who or what is approaching him.

humans, they respond well to praise and positive encouragement.

While recognising this, it has to be remembered that a horse views the world in a different way to a human. Being able to understand things from a horse's point of view is fundamental if a rider is going to achieve a partnership and harmony with the horse. This is an essential requirement for successful riding, whether your ambitions are simply to hack around the countryside safely, or to take part in a demanding equestrian sport such as eventing.

It is really quite amazing how many unnatural limitations Man expects modern horses to accept without question. For example, we confine our horses in individual stables from which they cannot escape; we provide them with feed at times we dictate; we expect them to accept our presence on their backs; we ride them in traffic; we shoe and clip them; and we expect them to walk into and travel happily in the confined spaces of trailers.

Instincts and memory

Consider how alien this lifestyle is to the horse's natural instincts. In the wild, horses live together in herds, free to move at their will and eating and drinking as they wish. As they are naturally nervous creatures, their instinct when faced with strange situations is to flee. Other defence mechanisms include bucking (for example when a predator lands on their back), kicking and biting.

The horse has been domesticated for centuries and could now be said to be conditioned to the way of life that humans have created for him. However, the animal's natural instincts have not been eradicated and examples of them can be seen every day.

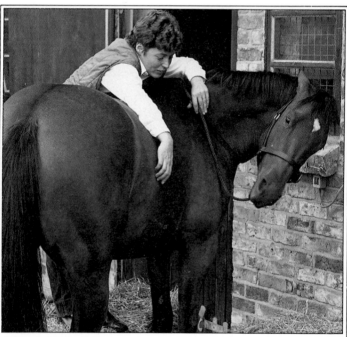

This youngster is being introduced to the strange phenomenon of having something on his back. Leaning over the horse in this way is a prelude to mounting. Look at the youngster's face – head whipped round, ears back, he has grabbed hold of the leadrope end in his mouth, all signs of his consternation at this new experience.

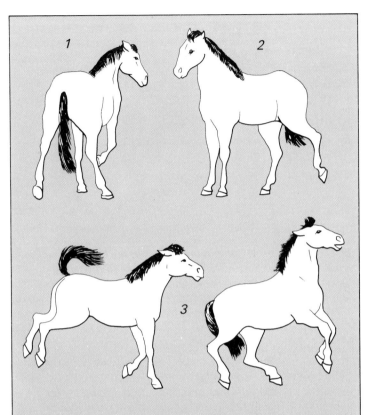

If a horse feels threatened he will let you, or other horses, know. The first stage of this warning system is generally shown by the ears being back, the tail clamped down and the horse moving his rump round to face whatever is threatening him (1). Some horses tend to show this phase when they are stabled and are given their feed. They are simply telling their owners that they prefer to eat in peace without anyone fussing around them. The second stage of this defensive warning would be a raised foot which shows that the horse is prepared to kick (2). Usually the threat of a kick is enough to make another horse back off. For example, when out hunting, horses often have to follow each other along headlands: if one gets too close for comfort to another horse, then a raised leg warns the horse (and the observant rider) to give more clearance. If all these warnings are ignored then a horse will kick (3).

These ponies have been living wild and are now facing something totally new for them – the sale ring. Despite having plenty of space they stick together and their body language reflects their confusion, ears back showing submission and fear, tight mouths indicating anxiety.

Take the herd instinct, which offers security to the horse. Go to any local show and you will see the pony or horse who is reluctant to leave the collecting ring and his own kind for the solitude of the jumping ring. Even those horses who are obedient and leave their friends, jump more keenly when going towards the collecting ring.

To stabled horses, the security offered by the herd in the wild has a substitute in the form of their stable. In the face of danger, such as stable fires, they are reluctant to leave their boxes.

Flight is another of their safety valves. There is the example of the young horse turned out in a field close to a railway line. The first time a train thunders past the youngster flies around the field. In time though, if regularly turned out in the field, he will become accustomed to the noisy trains, realise that they cannot harm him and so accept them as part of life.

However, if they associate a particular object or person with pain, then horses will continue to flee from it. For example, they have sensitive mouths and can be hurt easily by rough-handed riders. A horse may fight against a rider's rough treatment by taking off. As a result the rider uses a stronger bit, the horse pulls even more against the increased pain and thereby a vicious circle is created. In such cases, the solution is often to be found by changing to a milder bit, changing or totally re-educating the rider and then teaching the horse that there will be no pain and thus no need to flee.

Horses have very long memories for places, events and people. This can work either for or against their human companions. A sympathetic trainer or rider will use the horse's memory to his own benefit, in a very simple way – for example, always ending lessons on a good note so the horse associates learning with pleasure. Humans who are not so well 'tuned in' to horses will make such mistakes as letting the horse win, perhaps by refusing to jump a ditch or enter a stream. If the horse is allowed to get away with misbehaving, then he will be disobedient on other occasions, because his rider has let him be naughty.

When riding horses you need to give them as much opportunity as possible of doing what you ask. If they refuse, you need to establish why. Is it because of fear, confusion or naughtiness? Whatever the reason, then the problem must be

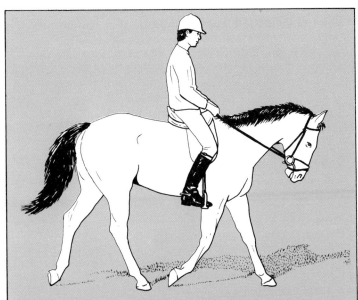

For successful riding you need to give the horse the best possible chance of doing what you ask – this includes having a good riding position yourself, understanding how and why the aids are applied, being clear in your riding objectives and being able to be self-critical when problems arise.

tackled sensibly and immediately. If allowed to fester, then a bigger and more difficult problem could result.

How the horse learns

It therefore makes sense for your horse to have a logical and progressive training programme. If a difficulty arises you can then go down a step and re-establish the basics before more difficult movements are attempted.

Horses learn through repetition and by being rewarded when good and reprimanded when naughty. However, like children, they must understand why they have been told off. To ask a horse to do something for which he is not yet ready, either mentally or physically, and then punish him for not complying, is totally wrong and unfair.

If you need help with a training sequence take a look at some recommended dressage tests (British Horse Society). You can see how the tests become progressively more difficult as the horse's training and education increase. You should bear in mind that not every horse can reach the advanced levels of dressage. A great deal of time and training goes into attaining such heights, and of course the individual horse's own natural ability, conformation and temperament play a part in how far he progresses.

This book is concerned primarily with 'ordinary' riders and/or owners, who often have to work full-time to keep their horses and who may enjoy competing at a local level, perhaps taking part in Preliminary and Novice dressage tests, unaffiliated novice events and so on. A little thought and consistent training can improve your horse's way of going – making him a more enjoyable ride.

Training the horse and rider

It follows that in trying to improve your horse, your own skills will also need refining. To be successful as a rider, it is imperative that you possess the ability to be self-critical. If you hit a problem with your horse's training, do not automatically blame the horse. If you do, without questioning your involvement in the partnership, then improvement will always elude you.

Take a step back and assess your riding or your handling of the situation, which may have created a problem. Is there

12

To fulfil his potential a horse needs to be relaxed, happy and confident. This extends further than being at one with his rider and includes other aspects of your horse's life such as his feeding, living space, general health and fitness. Successful riding involves being a good horsewoman or man in all senses, not just a capable rider.

anything you may have done, or indeed not done, which has initiated the problem or made it worse? In the majority of cases, it is rider error that has led to horse problems – for example, the rider's position or application of the aids.

Something that riders often forget is that horses are very sensitive to our moods and thoughts. If you are in a hurry there is no point in trying to school your horse. Your clockwatching and anxiety will be transferred to your horse who may react to all the urgency by being very onward-bound and difficult to settle. It is far better when you are in this frame of mind to hack out, rather than try to school which is sure to make matters worse.

Routine and regularity The way in which you handle your horse at all times will reflect upon his training programme. People who are always in a hurry, who rush jobs or become flustered, will not be able to develop a very satisfactory rapport with their horses, because they are not creating the type of environment that produces a relaxed, happy horse. There is no way that your horse can work well and confidently if he is uptight.

Routine is very important to horses, particularly where feeding is concerned. Failing to provide security through a routine results in stress, so again your horse will not be able to give of his best when he is ridden. Some people have better productivity rates in the mornings than afternoons, and horses are just the same. Establish whether your horse is a morning, afternoon or evening horse and then try to carry out an exercising and work routine around this.

The importance of confidence Never underestimate the power of your own thought either. If you convince yourself that you will never be able to remember a dressage test or undertake a certain movement, then you will not be able to do it. Banish those negative thoughts and tell yourself that you can improve. Negativity is a waste of time and energy, whereas positive thinking can result in tremendous achievements.

Your partner in sport will also benefit from your positive attitude. If a horse is a little uncertain when approaching a big fence he will derive confidence from a rider who sets to and attacks the fence rather than someone who just freezes and gives the horse no help or signals at all.

A loss of confidence can affect both horses and riders. Young horses who are asked to do too much too soon, whether on the flat or over jumps, may lose faith in themselves, and this can be manifested in several ways, such as a refusal to jump, nappiness or running off. In such instances, the value of a logical training plan is felt. By going back a few steps, re-establishing the basics and thereby restoring confidence, the problem is often overcome.

Horses of all ages can suffer crises of confidence. The difficulty may be momentary, as when, after suffering a fall, the horse may jump the next couple of fences rather stickily. However, positive riding from the rider can help to restore the horse's confidence.

Other crises need long-term treatment and in some cases may never be overcome. For instance, horses who have suffered unpleasant accidents in trailers can be forgiven for not wanting to enter a trailer again. However, most animals can have their confidence restored with time, patience and careful handling.

Humans have the advantage that they can reason for themselves when confidence crises occur. Having said that, even for humans, it can take just a few seconds to lose confidence and many weeks to restore it. Whatever the reason for your loss of confidence, be it a near-accident on the road, a bad fall over a jump or a terrifying experience such as being on a bolting horse, there is only one way to conquer your fear – and that is to face up to it and attack!

All riders, whether ordinary competitors or those who have

The only way to beat a confidence crisis is to face up to the problem and, with the help of a sympathetic instructor, attack your nerves, one step at a time. Falls are an occupational hazard; they happen to every rider, at every level. Do not allow your mind to magnify them out of all proportion.

represented their country, have at some time experienced a loss of confidence. Event rider Ginny Leng, who is an Olympic medallist, is one person who, having smashed her arm into many pieces in a horrible fall, considered her riding career. With superb horses like Priceless and Night Cap on the brink of their eventing careers, Ginny decided to return to the saddle and went on to claim many national and international honours.

The will to ride and to improve is present in all riders. You have to learn how to use it to your own advantage. Negative forces such as lack of confidence can be turned into positive assets. By admitting your fears, seeking help from sensitive instructors and tackling problems head on, one step at a time, you can regain your confidence. Of course it will take time, but, for instance, in overcoming a fear of jumping, you will have such a sense of personal triumph that the memory will stay with you and provide encouragement at times of any future setbacks.

Perhaps it is the numerous challenges offered by riding that make it such a satisfying and enjoyable sport. Horse riding tests your physical and mental abilities, your courage, your persistence and your common sense. In return it offers tremendous rewards, not the least of which is the sheer pleasure of being at one with a living creature.

It is important to be aware of the horse's nature at all times. Catching one horse with the aid of feed will only result in jealous and aggressive behaviour from his companions, putting you and your horse at risk.

CHAPTER TWO

Effective riding

If you watch a horse loose in a field you will see how easily he can twist and turn at all speeds, how quickly he can stop and how simple it is for him to accelerate from a standing start. However, this natural balance, agility and mobility are affected by the addition of a rider.

The effect of a rider is to place more weight on the horse's forehand. Take a look at any gathering of horses and riders and you will see horses moving around as if they are pulling themselves along from the front, rather than the driving force for their movement coming from their hindquarters. The outline or shape of such horses is long and low with their hocks trailing behind them.

Compare this image with that of the top dressage horses. Their shape or outline looks rounder, as if the horse can burst forwards effortlessly with energy into extravagant paces.

In order to carry a rider easily and move with maximum efficiency, a horse has to transfer some of the load, taking the strain of weight-bearing off the forehand and letting the hindquarters carry more weight. This can be achieved by the horse bringing his hocks further under the body, each of the horse's steps coming under the body as the hindquarters are engaged and providing propulsive power. The horse's back rounds, coming up to carry the weight of the rider.

The horse's natural centre of gravity is just behind the withers, roughly under the areas of the rider's knee and thigh. With the addition of a rider this centre of gravity moves forward slightly, placing more weight on the forehand, but by carrying more weight on the quarters the centre of gravity resumes its natural position and enables the horse to carry a rider while remaining agile and athletic.

As visits to local shows will demonstrate, not every horse moves as efficiently or carries a rider with as much ease as he might. Although not every animal has the potential to be a top dressage contender, each one can be improved and part of the challenge in riding lies in this search for improvement.

The rider's position

To help her horse, a rider must work on her own position. This is intended to help the horse as much as possible. For

17

instance, riders are told to sit in the deepest part of the saddle as this places them over the horse's natural centre of gravity. Unfortunately for the horse, not all riders adopt a good position, so they make life much more awkward for their mounts.

Riders who perch on their 'forks' instead of sitting in the saddle are putting more weight on the horse's forehand. If a rider sits too far back in the saddle he will feel much heavier to the horse. In this case the rider will be behind the centre of gravity but his 'extra' weight causes the horse to hollow its back; therefore, the hindquarters cannot come under the animal and thus the horse remains on the forehand.

If you do not take the trouble to develop a good riding position then your horse will be restricted both in his balance and also in his agility.

The flatwork riding position

So what makes for a decent riding position on the flat? When a horse jumps, his centre of gravity alters and the rider's position changes accordingly.

The basis of a good, effective position lies with a secure, independent seat. Think of the triangle made up by your two seatbones at the back and the fork of your thighbones at the front. When sitting correctly your weight will be in the middle of this triangle. In turn this will ensure that your pelvis is in the correct position with your hip joints open, allowing the legs the best chance of being in a good position.

Let your legs hang naturally around the horse's sides, lying as close as possible to the horse but without any tension. There will be a slight bend in your knees, toes pointing forwards and ankles at a slightly lower level than toes. The thighs need to be as flat as possible against the saddle so pull any spare muscle out and back.

Have your stirrup iron under the widest part of the foot, i.e. the ball, to give you more on which to balance. Think of your weight going down through your legs and then out, via supple ankles.

Sit tall in the saddle but without forcing your upper body into an upright, stiff position. You must keep a soft upper body so that you can absorb your horse's movement through your back and hips.

Look where you are going, let your arms hang easily by your sides with a bend at each elbow and flexibility in both

1 Maintaining a good position when the horse is stationary is easy enough but once the horse moves it is all too simple for something to go wrong. Here the rider is executing a rising trot but still keeping the required vertical line through ears, shoulder, hip and heel.

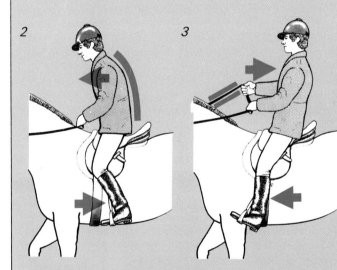

2 A common fault is to tip forwards, which results in a rounding of the back so the seat cannot be used as effectively; and a drawing back of the leg, again reducing the rider's ability to apply any aids in the correct place.
3 An insecure seat is shown by the rider using the reins for balance whilst the position also collapses. Leaning back results in the lower legs being thrust forwards.

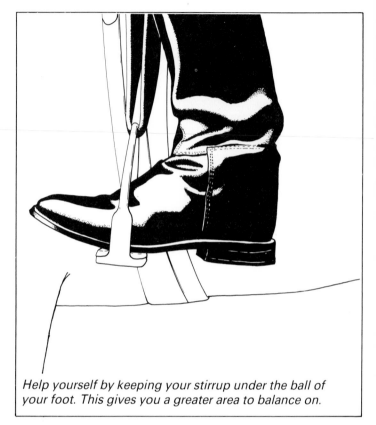

Help yourself by keeping your stirrup under the ball of your foot. This gives you a greater area to balance on.

the shoulders and elbows so that you can follow easily the movement of the horse's head and neck.

There should be a straight line from your elbow, through your wrist and hand to the reins and the horse's mouth. Carry your hands about three inches above the horse's withers with the thumbs uppermost as if you were reading a book. Make sure that the hands are level and the wrists slightly bent. It helps to create a more sympathetic hand if you think of your hands and arms as belonging to the horse.

When viewed from the side it should be possible to draw an imaginary straight line through your ear, shoulder, hip and heel. If your position is not in alignment then it will not be as secure or effective. A check for correct leg position is the position of the stirrup leather, which should be perpendicular to the ground. From a front or back view the rider should be sitting straight and upright and not have either 'collapsed' shoulders or hips.

Balance and communication

The rider's position should be balanced and free of tension. Only in an emergency should he or she resort to gripping with knees or thighs. As the horse moves so the rider needs to maintain her position and herein lie potential problems. The

Only by becoming supple will you be able to absorb the movement of your horse through your back and hips. Mounted and dismounted exercises, performed for a few minutes each day, will result in improved suppleness and a generally improved fitness level.

The imaginary line from hip to heel also serves as a useful indicator for the 'target' range for the lower leg aid. If an aid is applied behind the line indicated then it will be on an area of the horse where the intercostal nerve, the 'magic' spot, is well covered by flesh and muscle, so the effectiveness of the aid is greatly reduced. This rider would benefit from placing the foot further in the stirrup so that the iron was on the ball of the foot.

horse's movement needs to be absorbed via the waist and lumbar area, so the rider must be supple. Lack of suppleness creates tension leading to resistance on the horse's part, which shows up in a poor outline, hollowed back, and a raised head and neck.

As the riding position is designed to allow for effective communication between horse and rider, it follows that a sudden change in the rider's position will result in impaired communication. For example, if a rider's pelvis is tipped back there is too much weight on the seat bones, the legs come forward and the rider's back becomes rounded. Apart from being more difficult to communicate with the horse, the rider will also find it harder to absorb the horse's movement and stay in balance.

Sitting crookedly presents even greater and longer-term problems for both horse and rider. If a rider sits crookedly for a

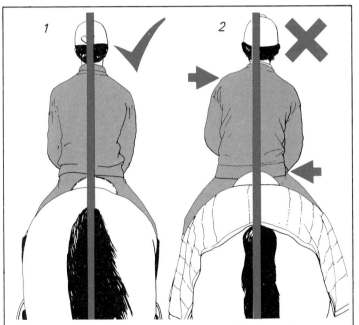

1 Ask your instructor or a friend to check your riding position from behind.

2 Here the rider is sitting slightly unlevel. Her right-hand side is taking more weight than the left-hand side, and this will affect how her horse moves.

Whatever your level of riding ability, lessons on the lunge will improve both your seat and position.

long period then the horse will try to match this by moving with his quarters to one side, probably moving better on one rein than the other, and will start to build up the wrong muscles.

Constantly sitting crookedly can actually put a horse's back out of alignment or, at the least, make the animal sore. Horses with back problems tell us of their pain by moving unlevel, by hollowing and, if in severe pain, by refusing to do certain tasks like jumping.

Riders should be aware that if they have been sitting crookedly for a long period it can feel wrong for some time after their position has been corrected. As with horses, it takes time to correct one-sidedness in the rider.

Lungeing the rider

It is worth investing in some regular lunge lessons to help your riding. If you wish to overcome a particular problem, a series of short 20-minute sessions, say three times a week, will help to bring about an improvement. Beware of sessions

24

that last for too long as working on the lunge is extremely strenuous, and carrying on when the muscles are over-tired can bring about further problems.

Even if you feel that you have no specific problems, regular lunge lessons will improve your seat, balance, suppleness, strength, appreciation of the horse's movement, understanding and application of the aids and your general approach as a 'thinking rider'.

Lungeing a horse and rider so that benefits are derived from the exercises, is a particular skill. Do not be tempted to ask an inexperienced friend to help; it is far wiser to seek expert tuition. The lunge horse is as important as the instructor. Most reputable schools will have suitable animals which are well trained and used to the task. Young or immature animals should not be used for ridden lunge work as it is too demanding for them and may result in injury.

Lungeing also has other uses: horses are lunged without riders, as part of their training programme, or for exercise if their owner cannot undertake normal mounted exercise.

Exercises for suppleness and agility

Dismounted exercises to help your riding agility also bring you benefits in the shape of general fitness and well-being. Here is a selection for you to try:

Head rolls Let your chin rest on your chest and then slowly

If you want to improve the strength in your legs this is a good exercise. Sit on an imaginary chair, using a wall as the chair back. Holding this position for a few seconds is painful enough at first! It helps if you can take your mind off the pain by reading or talking while maintaining this position.

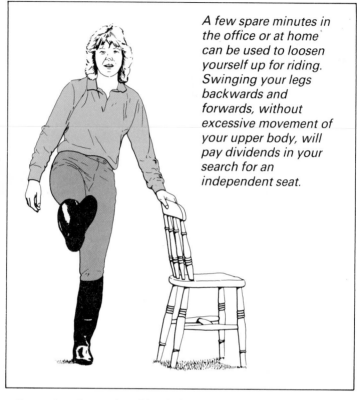

A few spare minutes in the office or at home can be used to loosen yourself up for riding. Swinging your legs backwards and forwards, without excessive movement of your upper body, will pay dividends in your search for an independent seat.

roll your head round and back, in both clockwise and anticlockwise directions.

Shoulder hunches Lift both shoulders as if you are trying to touch your ears with them. Roll the shoulders backwards and downwards.

Arms Work the shoulder, elbow and wrist joints by holding your arms out to the side with your palms facing up to the ceiling. Now turn your arms the right way round, then 'inside out' and so on.

Arm rotations Circle the arms slowly, individually and then together.

Body Stand with your feet at a shoulders' width apart, keeping your lower body as still as possible, swivel your upper body to the left, then to the right and repeat.

Side stretches Stand with your legs comfortably apart – do not tip forwards. Stretch your left hand down your left leg as far as possible without being uncomfortable, then try the right hand down the right leg and repeat.

Toe touching Stand with your feet apart, touch the left toe with the right hand, return to the upright position and then touch your right toe with the left hand. If you cannot manage to reach your feet at first, stretch down as far as you can. Practise and you will eventually succeed!

Ankles Sit at your office desk and rotate your ankles to increase their suppleness.

Mounted exercises will include some of the above exercises along with movements such as touching the horse's ears and tail, raising both knees above the saddle so you feel your seatbones, and holding the legs out from the sides of the saddle. Executed at halt, walk and trot, these can be quite difficult to master – they will certainly result in aching muscles but the thought to keep you going is that they will definitely help your riding!

From this position this rider can lift her knees upwards so that she can feel her seatbones. Lifting the knees up and then holding the legs out from the saddle is another strengthening exercise.

Common positional faults

A poor seat can originate in a number of ways such as a wrongly positioned body or legs, or a general lack of confidence and comfort. Some of these problems and their solutions are listed below. Tenseness can be caused by:

● The rider trying too hard, particularly if he or she is working towards a specific competition and is seeking perfection.
● A fall that has resulted in fear and loss of confidence.
● The rider being worried about external problems at home or at work, and not being able to switch off and concentrate on riding.
● A strange horse who is perhaps more forward-going than the rider's usual mount.

Another common positional fault is the rider's upper body tipping forwards. This can be caused by one of the following:
● An insecure seat – the weight not properly distributed through the seat bones, and rounding of the shoulders and the back.
● Fear or nervousness.

The lower legs swinging forwards or back is another positional fault. This is usually caused by:
● An insecure seat with the weight unevenly distributed.

The solutions

Restoring riding confidence takes time, especially if the rider has experienced a really bad fall. Patient instructors, quiet horses and a determination on the part of riders to conquer their fear, are vital for success. Nervous riders must be taken back to basics (how far back depends on individual circumstances) and then encouraged, or occasionally bullied gently, into taking small steps.

Lunge lessons will often help here, as they will for riders who are trying to adapt to new horses. Developing a secure and independent seat will give riders the confidence to ride by balance, and to know that they can sit horses without having to resort to gripping fiercely with knees, thighs and calves in order to stay on.

The more riding you do, the more confidence you will gain and the more relaxed you will become, which is vital if you are to achieve harmony with the horse.

General positional advice

A rider's position can be affected by her own body shape, by the saddle used, the shape of her horse and her occupation. Short, round riders will naturally find it more difficult to stretch their legs down and around their horse, whereas tall, slim people find it relatively easy to adopt a reasonable leg position. You need to be aware of your own body and how it helps or restricts your riding. Some elements, such as your weight, can be altered to bring about an improvement whereas you need to learn how to make the most of things that cannot be altered.

Women riders have an advantage over males in that the shape of their pelvis makes it easier for them to achieve a

The search for a good seat necessitates hard work, exercising both off and on the horse. For mounted exercises pull the buckle of the stirrup leathers away from the bar so that you can cross your stirrups without undue bulk on which to bruise your legs.

deeper seat. They have a broader base of support as there is greater distance beween the seat bones and they also have a wider pubic arch.

The size and conformation of the horse will have an effect upon the rider's position. For instance, a tall, slim rider mounted on a small and narrow horse will result in the rider's legs being too far below the horse's belly so it is impossible for her to apply any leg aids correctly. This may sound obvious but it is surprising how many horses and riders are mis-matched.

Saddles should fit both horse and rider. If they do not fit the horse they can cause rubbing or restrict the horse's movement; alternatively, if the saddle is not suitable for the rider then it could result in her balance being affected, or it may not be large enough to offer sufficient contact between the saddle and the rider's seat or legs.

Riders who have rather sedentary jobs, maybe sitting behind an office desk all day, will find that this reflects on their riding. Stiffness can be a problem as can rounded backs when people are crouched over a desk. Take a look at your daily routine and lifestyle and how they affect your riding.

It is clear that many riders' problems stem from their seat, so for successful riding it is vital that time is spent on this first basic step of achieving a good and effective position. Once this is established, the rider can move on. If this foundation is neglected, then there will be no firm base from which to build and the cracks are bound to appear sooner or later in your riding career.

The aids

The way in which a rider communicates her wishes to a horse is very important. The lines of communication are through the *natural aids*; which are the rider's seat, legs, hands, voice and thoughts, and the *artificial aids* such as whips, spurs and martingales.

For a horse to understand what is required of him the rider's instructions must be crystal clear. If the rider is not sure what she wants, then the horse has no chance of obliging!

The aids do not operate as separate entities but are used in a co-ordinated way, the sequence being preparation by thought and planning followed by seat, legs, then hands. It is important for you to be able to use each hand and leg independently, because as you progress, you will learn that

Although this rider looks quite relaxed and confident on his horse, the fact that he is sitting too far back will reduce his chances of being an effective rider. As he is not sitting in the central part of the saddle his legs are too far back, even though he has managed to maintain a straight line from his ear through to his heel.

there are subtle degrees of application of the aids. For instance, a wide range of leg aids can be used from a press to a nudge or a kick.

Horses that are trained to a high level have a large 'vocabulary' as far as aids are concerned, and this is why so many less experienced riders, when mounted on advanced horses, fail to get much response from their mounts. In such cases, horses and riders are communicating on different levels. Riders need to know how to use their aids and be able to use them without getting the lines of communication to the horse tangled. All too often, they are seen kicking with their legs while their hands and bodies are firmly resisting any forward movement by the horse!

When talking about the riding position, the importance of the seat was stressed. Everything flows from a good seat. For example, riders who are secure and confident are able to use their hands sensitively, because they do not need to balance on the reins.

The weight aids

The use of a rider's weight is also extremely important.
Through the sensitive use of her weight aids, a rider can
execute turns and circles without actually needing to use the
reins at all. When moving on a straight line the rider's weight
is central. If she wishes to turn left, then by moving the left
seat bone forwards a fraction, before giving any other
instructions, the rider is inviting the horse to turn.

This shift of weight must not be over-exaggerated or the
rider will sit crookedly. On a circle, think of moving the inner
hip forwards and of sitting firmly on the inside seat bone, and
very lightly on the outside seat bone. Such movements do
require considerable suppleness and refinement from the
rider, and these can be achieved only through riding
experience along with good-quality instruction. An adviser on
the ground is essential to avoid developing faults such as
collapsed hips, leaning in, or dropped shoulders in your
attempts to use your weight aids.

The leg aids

Basically, the rider's legs are the principal driving aid. That is
to say, they create movement, primarily forwards, but also
sideways and backwards, remembering, of course, that other
aids are used along with the legs to produce such
movements.

Your legs should always be in contact with your horse so
that you maintain a 'conversation' with him. As you walk
around an enclosed area be aware of the feel of the horse's
flank against your leg. You should maintain a light contact via
your leg with the horse at all times. If you wish the horse to
increase his speed then you close your legs 'on the girth'
around the horse. In effect, the horse feels the rider's legs
squeezing him and reacts by moving away from the squeezing
motion.

Where you apply your leg aids is important. The horse has a
'magic spot' known as the intercostal nerve which, when
activated, sets off an arching reaction in his back and brings
the hindleg further forwards. The nerve can be found about
half-way between the horse's elbow and the saddle flap.
Although further along the flank it is covered by muscles and
flesh, the magic spot is most sensitive at a point just in front

32

of the saddle girth. Leg aids that are given close to this point, i.e., on, just in front of or just behind the girth, will therefore be more effective. The use of the legs in front of the girth is the domain of the more experienced rider who is trying to obtain more extension and is not really applicable here.

Everyone has seen the rider who draws her leg way back and kicks madly, but to no avail. Little wonder really, for she is not on target and is not stimulating the horse.

The leg aids may be used in various ways, such as alternately, as in walking, when you are trying to encourage the horse to walk out more; distinct pressure with both legs as you might when asking the horse to perform an acute transition; or short, and squeezing lightly in rhythm, for example when trotting.

Drawing the leg back and bringing the heel up to apply an aid is a common fault. Tall riders often bring their heels up to give leg aids. They should be made aware of this and apply themselves to correcting the fault.

The rider's legs also regulate movement. For example, when performing sideways moves, such as turns on the forehand, the horse will move away from the rider's leg that is applying more pressure, although the rider must maintain sufficient pressure with her other leg to prevent the horse from walking forwards.

Once the horse has reacted to your leg aid, the pressure should be reduced but the conversation between your legs and your horse remains. This communication between horse and rider also has the purpose of giving the horse confidence. Remember that the aids should be applied with the inside of your lower leg, not the back of your heel. Your aids are intended to influence your horse and the best time to do this is as the horse's hind leg comes off the ground because if an

Another common fault is that of turning the toe out with the result that the rider is unable to use the whole of the lower leg to apply an aid.

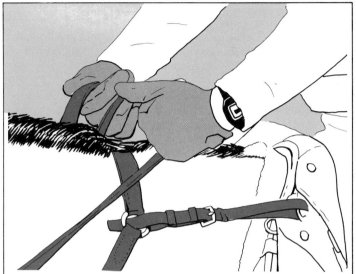

Rounding the wrists results in a tense wrist and lower arm, so the rider's lines of communication with the horse's mouth are inevitably adversely affected.

aid is applied at precisely the correct moment its influence will be to bring the leg further underneath the horse.

Use of the hands

The last of the aids to be used are the hands, although unfortunately too many riders use them excessively and too soon. Keep in the forefront of your mind that the sequence of the aids is seat, legs and *then* hands.

Through the hands the rider has access to an extremely sensitive part of the horse – his mouth. It is very easy to damage or deaden a horse's mouth through poor use of the hands. A rider's hands are meant to receive and regulate the impulsion created by the legs, not act as a rough and ready means of stopping. Your fingers should open to let the horse move forwards, if that is what your legs have asked him to do, or close around the rein to restrain or reduce forward movements.

The way in which you apply your rein aids also enables you to re-channel some of the energy created. For turns and circles open reins may be used, especially when training young horses, which means that the rein is carried off the neck, with the hand held slightly outwards in the direction of the movement. This is also known as a direct rein aid. A rein can also be used to prevent forward movement, as it is for rein-backs, to move the horse's quarters or shoulders, or to move the whole horse sideways.

Remember that your hands act in co-operation with each other. One hand may be guiding the horse, while the other is regulating the pace and supporting your leg aids. Keep your hands steady. Do not move them up and down, but do yield to, and keep a good contact with, the horse's mouth, matching what he gives you.

One way of thinking about your contact is to imagine that your have a live bird in your hand. You should be holding it firmly enough to prevent it escaping but not so much that you crush the creature. Stiff arms can lead to problems because the horse will feel the tension in his mouth and will react by

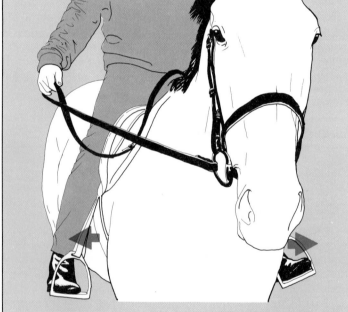

Demonstrating the use of an open rein, eg., as it is applied for turns and circles. However, in concentrating on the rein, the rider has taken her lower leg off the horse so the pattern of communication through the seat, legs and hands has been disrupted.

inactive paces, head throwing or tilting and generally being unsettled in his mouth, perhaps grinding the bit.

Artificial aids

In this context, spurs, whips and martingales are included. Other schooling 'aids' or gadgets do exist but are better left to more experienced riders, as their inexpert use can do more harm than good.

Spurs are an effective way of improving and refining a horse's response to your leg aids but if abused, the result can be the ruination of your horse's training. If worn, spurs should lie along the top seam of the heel of the boot, so that with the legs in the correct position the spurs are not in contact with the horse. If the rider wishes to use her spur she has to turn her toe out slightly. Spurs should not be worn unless you have already achieved an independent seat and good control of your legs!

Schooling whips are carried with the knob pushed down to the hand and are held lightly across the rider's thigh. They can be difficult to handle because of their length, but once control of the schooling whip is mastered it is useful for backing up your leg aids. The most common fault is for riders to inadvertently flick their horses with their whips because their hands are unsteady.

Check your whip regularly, as it is quite easy for the end to come off, and this can result in a cut horse. Insulating tape wound around the end offers some protection until a new whip can be purchased.

Martingales are used on horses who try to evade their riders' instructions by raising their heads in the air and thereby making it difficult for the rider to successfully apply any aids.

Running martingales are the most commonly used; these consist of a neckstrap joined to a piece of leather which attaches to the girth at one end and divides into two at the other end. These two pieces of leather have rings on the end, through which the reins pass. When correctly fitted, the martingale has no effect while the horse maintains a reasonable head position, but if he tries to throw his head in the air then downward pressure is exerted through the reins.

CHAPTER THREE

Problem solving

Before you can hope to achieve anything with your horse he must be obedient. Hopefully his training will have followed a logical sequence and will have used the tenets of reward and punishment, mixed with compassion and horse sense, so that the horse understands what is expected of him and obeys his rider's instructions.

Use the aids correctly

Ideally your aids shoud be applied so that they are barely visible. If your horse needs a hefty kick in the ribs to get him started, then you should work on his obedience to light aids before trying to progress any further.

You can improve your horse's acceptance of light aids by giving him a reminder with the stick if he does not react to an aid. However, first you must be quite sure that your horse understands what is required of him and that you have applied the aid clearly and correctly.

If, for instance, you ask your horse to walk on and he does not budge, do not increase the severity of your aid but ask again, and this time if he does not react, back up your aid with a flick of your whip. Schooling whips should be carried for flatwork, as it is possible to issue a reminder without having to remove the whip hand from the rein.

Make sure that you insist on this policy of reacting quickly to light aids at all times. Such consistency will result in your horse being obedient and responsive to light aids. This is preferable to constantly nagging or niggling away with your legs, which only results in a horse who is 'deadened' to the effect and simply ignores you.

Move on to forwards movement

Once you have obedience, then you can concentrate on forwards movement. It is vital that at all paces the horse works and thinks forwards. Remember that transitions are also forward movements – for example, the horse comes down from a trot forwards into a walk: he does *not* fall out of a trot into a slovenly wander along!

38

Discipline is needed to ensure that your horse's standard of schooling improves. Obedience to light aids is vital and must be established before trying to improve further with a training programme for your horse.

The forward movement must be at the speed dictated by the rider, it will be generated by the rider's legs and contained or controlled by the rider's sympathetic hands. Riders should not worry about getting their horse on the bit – think first of all of obedience, then of forwards movement. These must be firmly established in the horse's training before any more serious demands can be made. A horse is on the bit when he moves in balance and rhythm, and with active forward movement from the rider's legs into an elastic contact with the bit. The hindquarters are engaged, the outline is round, the poll is the highest point of the neck and the head is carried steady. Your horse needs to have a supple flexing jaw and to be in self-carriage. To test self-carriage, for instance in canter, establish the canter and then surrender the reins, i.e., give up contact and stretch your hands forwards so that there are loops in the reins. If the horse is in self-carriage, he will continue without altering his pace or his position, which means that his outline will not suddenly become 'long'.

If you have difficulty establishing whether or not the horse is going forwards sufficiently, in the walk for example, you should ask yourself the question: 'Is the horse walking for himself or will the next stride be a stop 'stride'? If the answer is that he is going to stop, then he is not going forwards enough and you need to generate more movement through the use of your legs and a correspondingly sensitive hand.

A common fault with riders is a lack of quality where their contact with the horse is concerned. This was discussed under riding position (see page 17). Remember that if you have too strong a contact you will restrict your horse's movement but if it is insufficient then any impulsion you generate will immediately be lost out of the 'front door'. For example, you may ask for a canter. If the horse has an active trot and the rider has sufficient contact, then when the aids are applied a canter strike-off will be achieved. If the rider has only a sloppy contact, then the chances are that the horse will simply trot faster when asked to canter. This is because there is nothing, i.e., no contact, for the horse to go forwards into, and hence any impulsion generated escapes – in this case, in the form of a faster trot.

Riding with rhythm

With obedience and free forward movement established, it is time to think of rhythm. Throughout all his gaits your horse should work rhythmically. As a rider it will help your 'feel' considerably if you start to count out your horse's strides in all his work. Say them out loud at first and then to yourself. Do this all the time and it is amazing how much more you can understand about what is happening as the horse walks, trots and canters. Counting out strides also makes you prepare for movements to a greater degree than usual with the result that this movement often turns out better.

To achieve lengthened strides, the rider must generate more impulsion but still contain the horse's front end so that the extra energy is used in an increased length of stride rather than the horse simply moving faster. Here you can see that the horse is still working in a reasonable outline. Compare this with the picture below.

Instead of lengthening his stride, the horse is running on, with all the excess impulsion being lost through the front end. His head has lifted and he has lost the roundness of outline seen in the picture above.

If your horse can maintain a good rhythm then he is in balance. Remember that the rhythm of the pace should be kept through turns and corners. To achieve this you may need to use stronger leg aids throughout such movements.

You can also count out strides while hacking. Count the number of strides between telegraph poles and then try to add or subtract strides as an exercise. This can also be done along the long side of a manege.

Alternatively, place two white or coloured poles about 20 yards (18 metres) apart on the centre line of your schooling area. Work over the poles in trot and canter, counting the number of strides, then lengthening or shortening your horse's stride between the poles. Do not use rustic poles, as these are more difficult for the horse to see.

During this work on lengthening and shortening strides your horse must maintain even, rhythmic strides. Young horses may find the exercises difficult at first until they become more aware of the positioning of their feet.

Whatever you plan to do with your horse in the future, an important thread throughout his work is evenness of stride. If your horse hunts, show jumps, events or races, an evenness

This horse is very much on his forehand, a natural way of going for the species. His hindlegs are trailing and he lacks the springy, elastic steps and round outline of a horse whose hindquarters are engaged.

of stride helps you to reduce your chances of meeting a fence incorrectly.

Another 'stride and rhythm' exercise for riders is to work the horse at a canter, stand for six strides, and then sit for six strides. This helps to strengthen your legs as well as improving your balance and feel.

Your horse's outline follows on from the first three of obedience, forwards movement and rhythm. Do not attempt to force your horse into an outline until these prerequisites are obtained and established, otherwise you will create more problems for yourself.

The objectives of schooling

A well-schooled horse will be active in his hindquarters so that his hindlegs are coming through from behind and are being placed well under the body generating impulsion, harnessed active forwards movement. His back is round and active; the forehand is light; he is accepting contact with the bit and is obedient to the aids.

A horse can only be truly on the bit when he has a supple, flexing jaw, is balanced and in self-carriage. Time, patience

A reasonable example of a working trot with the horse coming through from behind, working in a good outline and accepting the contact.

and logical schooling are needed to reach this stage. It is certainly worth finding a good instructor to assist with your flatwork training, especially if you have a young horse.

For instance, you may start by trying to teach a youngster to accept contact with the bit in walk whereas the best pace to work in, in this instance, is trot. By attempting this important part of training in a gait that has little natural impulsion, the result is likely to be a horse who raises his head artificially, hollows his back and works behind the bit.

The importance of a knowledgeable trainer on the ground cannot be over-emphasised. If you seriously want to progress with your horse, then make sure that you include instruction in your horse budget.

Naturally, the horse carries about sixty per cent of his weight on his forehand and forty per cent on his hindquarters. Throughout your horse's training, you are trying to encourage him to accept your weight and carry more of the overall weight on his hindquarters. As the level of the horse's training progresses so this becomes even more important, and at the higher levels of dressage you can see how the horse is extremely collected – for example, as in the piaffe.

The magnificent white horses of the Spanish Riding School in Vienna, who uphold the finest traditions of classical equitation and are an inspiring sight for any rider.

Although the purpose of this book is to assist riders during the earlier stages of their horse's training, it is useful to appreciate the high standards that can be achieved with some horses given time and training. One of the best examples of classical equitation is, or course, the Spanish Riding School of Vienna which periodically visits Britain and gives displays. If you can ever attend such a display, you will see riders and horses as one – truly poetry in motion.

The walk

The walk is a four-time gait with four distinct and even beats to every stride. The sequence of steps is quite complicated compared with the other gaits. As the horse's engine is his hindquarters, the first step taken when a horse moves off into walk will be with a hindleg. For instance, the sequence could

Even though he is walking on a long rein, this horse is moving actively, with distinct, even steps.

be nearside hind, nearside fore, offside hind and offside fore. A horse with a good walk will swing his back and neck.

A horse's walk is the most difficult gait to develop and the easiest to ruin. In a horse's training you should work on the other paces before trying to establish the walk. Most of your horse's work will be done in medium walk, i.e., when the horse is working well from behind, with free energetic strides, his hindfeet coming down over the tracks left by the forefeet, and he is accepting the rein.

Free walk is used to reward the horse – the rider allows the horse to stretch down and take the bit, still maintaining a contact. The horse's steps are long and rhythmical but they should not be lazy.

The other two forms of walk are collected and extended but these are outside the scope of this book, as are the collected and extended variants in other paces. A horse's natural ability will determine whether or not he can perform variations of pace such as collection and extension. Initially a horse has neither the impulsion, suppleness nor balance to collect or extend. Therefore early work is generally executed in what are termed working paces. These require the horse to stay in

46

balance, work actively from the hocks and quarters so that impulsion is generated, and stay in a reasonable outline.

Before trying to assess your horse's walk spend time getting to understand the feel and rhythm of the gait. Work in an enclosed area and count out the beats of the walk. The horse should lift and put down each leg separately. If he is dragging his feet, then either the rider is being slovenly, and this is being transmitted to the horse, or there is a veterinary problem that needs attention.

As he walks, the horse's steps should each be of the same length. Your horse should move in a free, easy rhythm, with unhurried strides. To balance himself your horse will nod his head and you must follow this movement with your hands and arms. Restricting it will lead to a poorer walk with shortened steps.

Your horse should step forward confidently into your hand. However, you can affect his ability or aptitude to do this through an ineffective or poor riding position. Riders who

As the rider is not using her position to push the horse on up to his bridle, so the long rein walk has become inactive, the steps have lost their length and elasticity, and the combination looks more as if it is going to stop than stride on confidently.

'droop' on their horses, that is to say who sit sloppily without any rein contact, encourage their horses to amble along instead of walking out.

On the other hand, riding with stiff, straight arms which are unyielding to the horse, results in an upset animal who shows his displeasure by raising his head, perhaps tipping it to one side, opening his mouth and swishing his tail.

Riders of horses who are lazy in the walk must beware of hurrying the horse so much that they destroy his natural stride and balance. It is best to do any work on walk when out on a hack as the horse is more likely to be relaxed and there is a purpose to his walk.

If your horse's walk is poor it could be because he has never learnt to swing his back. Work the horse in trot and canter first, then come back to walk and encourage the horse to stretch down and lengthen his neck (i.e., work him on a circle, asking him to lower his neck by gently giving and taking with the inside rein). Make sure that your arms and hands are ready to follow the movement of the horse's head

Now the rider shows, by surrendering her contact, how the horse takes advantage, raises his head, hollows his outline and consequently takes shorter steps.

as he relaxes. Then work on three loop serpentines in walk to encourage the hindlegs to swing forward as you change direction. Gradually your horse will learn to swing his back and lengthen his steps.

If your horse hurries along, breaking into a jog rather than walking rhythmically, then work on circles, figures of eight and constant changes of direction, aiming to direct more of his energy into forward motion instead of wasted 'up and down' movements. Use half-halts to gain his attention and re-balance him.

Half-halts

A half-halt is a signal from the rider to the horse that effectively attracts the horse's attention, as if to say to him 'Now listen, we're about to do something'. The effect of the half-halt is to re-engage the hindquarters, re-balance the horse, lighten the forehand and enhance his rhythm.

To achieve this the rider sits in the saddle, closes both legs firmly around the horse, using sufficient leg to ensure that the hocks are kept underneath the horse, and squeezes firmly on

To prepare a horse for a canter transition a rider may feel that it is necessary to give a half-halt so that the horse's attention is gained and his hindquarters are re-engaged.

*Showing the diagonal, two-time movement of the trot:
here the horse is going well, although he is not quite
round enough in his outline.*

the outside rein while still maintaining the bend in the
direction of the movement with the inside rein.

A half-halt is given, followed by the aids for the particular
movement you wish to do.

The trot

This is the best pace to use for schooling; it is the easiest one
in which to establish rhythm because of the two-time
symmetrical movement of the trot. The horse's legs move in
diagonal pairs, the right diagonal (off-fore and near-hind
together) and the left diagonal (near-fore and off-hind
together). In between there is a moment of suspension as the
horse springs from one diagonal to another.

Beginners to riding find the trot bouncy at first because of
this springing from one diagonal pair of legs to the other.
Riders may sit to the trot trying to absorb the movement
through their back and hips or rise, i.e., rise and sit on
alternate diagonals.

Ideally the horse should move with light, elastic steps that are rhythmical and unhurried. His quarters should be engaged and he should be flexing his joints, not dragging his limbs along.

Lack of activity in the trot is a common problem, usually because the rider has not yet learnt the correct balance between the hand and leg to produce the required pace.

Once again, the rider's position can affect the horse's trot. By leaning back, with stiff arms and balancing on the reins, a rider disturbs his horse's rhythm and balance. The result is that the horse raises his head and neck, hollows his back and thereby finds it difficult to stride out actively.

Another common fault is for the rider to have insufficient contact so that the horse falls on to his forehand and drags himself along rather than using his quarters to propel his body forwards.

Compare this photograph with the preceding one and it is quite clear how a rider's position can totally disrupt a horse's balance and rhythm. This rider is demonstrating the effect of pulling herself up by her hands and having a tense body. Her horse is reacting with a raised head, hollow back and shortened steps. His objections to the way the rider is communicating with him are also seen in his swishing tail, open mouth and the position of his ears.

For your schooling sessions aim for a good working trot in which the horse's hindlegs are active and are stepping well underneath him. He should be going forwards confidently into the rider's hand with swinging, even steps, a steady head and a slight swing in the back.

From this you can lengthen the strides so that your horse is working in medium trot. The rider increases the activity of the hindquarters through the leg aids but does not allow the horse to run on or quicken the rhythm. The forehand must still be light and the steps of the trot should lengthen.

Although this horse's hindleg is coming well underneath him, he is not going forwards confidently into his rider's hands. Look at the resistance shown by his ears and open mouth. Because she is holding her hands too high, this rider will be unable to encourage the horse to drop his nose and become rounder. The rider's legs are not as effective as they could be as she seems to be reaching for her stirrups.

The canter

The rolling sensation of the canter is created by the three-time beat of the gait. The movement starts with a hindleg, for example, the near-hind for a 'right' canter, and as this comes under the horse there is a raising of the forehand and lowering of the quarters. Then the off-hind and near-fore, i.e. left diagonal, make the second beat. The off-fore is beat three and as this is the leading foreleg and the only one on the ground, so the forehand lowers and the quarters raise. A moment of suspension follows before the sequence starts again.

Although this pace is the one that horses find most natural, a young horse trying to cope with having a rider on his back and cantering as well, finds it difficult to balance.

More experienced horses, however, should canter in balance, with even strides, in rhythm and with impulsion. A lack of impulsion will be shown by the horse appearing to nod excessively. It will also be difficult to hear the three

This canter started with the near-hind, and here we can see that the second beat, the diagonal pair of legs, is about to come into contact with the ground.

distinct beats; usually the diagonal pair breaks down into two separate beats if there is insufficient impulsion.

The horse should be straight. If you have mirrors in an arena you can see whether your horse's quarters are out of line. Alternatively, check that the prints of the hindfeet follow in the tracks of the forefeet or ask a friend or your instructor to watch as you travel along the long side. Using the latter method your adviser will also be able to see whether you are sitting crookedly or not.

The gallop is a faster version of the canter, although the diagonal sequence of the canter is broken so that the gallop is four-time.

Upward and downward transitions

Transitions are changes of pace, with the horse finding upward transitions easier than downward ones. This is because the horse is better designed for moving faster than slowing down (remember that flight was the horse's best defence mechanism in the wild).

Your transition will be affected by the quality of the pace *before* the transition. If you have a good, active, balanced trot, then the chances are that your transition into canter will be a smooth one. However, trying to canter when all that your horse is doing is running faster on the forehand, instead of trotting properly, is a recipe for a disastrous transition.

Preparation is vital. Make sure that your horse is well balanced with plenty of impulsion and 'listening' to your legs. Sit down in the saddle, have your legs firmly on your horse's sides and push him away from underneath you. Maintain a good contact with your horse's mouth and resist the temptation to lean forward as you try to make the transition into a faster pace. You must stay in balance with your horse as he steps into his new pace.

In Chapter 2 we referred to the importance of keeping a conversation going with your horse. Your legs should always be in contact with his sides so that any signal from you is not a shock. If your horse is onward bound it is tempting to keep your legs away from his sides, but when you ask for a transition your horse is likely to react to your sudden request by going hollow in his back, leading to shortened steps, resistance and a poor transition.

When mounted on a lazy horse it is a common fault of riders to tip forward ahead of the horse as he makes the transition.

This is normally accompanied by a loss of contact so the horse has nothing to go forward into and falls into the transition and pace.

Of all the transitions, that from trot to canter tends to magnify faults the most. Whether the rider is too restrictive or too sloppy, all will be revealed by the horse's mannerisms. Resistant or unhappy signs include the raising of head and neck; hollowing of the back; swishing tail; shortened steps; open mouth; unsteady head carriage and general facial expressions such as ears back and eyes rolling.

For the canter transition the rider should stay upright so that the forehand can remain light. If you tip forward or to the side you will unbalance your horse, possibly even causing stumbling.

Transitions from trot to canter magnify problems as this rider demonstrates for us. The fact that she is twisting in the saddle and gripping up with her leg upsets her horse, who is used to his rider sitting in balance and harmony with him. He shows his displeasure and the resulting transition is poorer because the horse has been distracted.

Downward transitions present more problems for the horse, as he tends to fall on to his forehand. Nature intends horses to take the strain of stopping on their hind legs, which have flexible hock joints, but with the extra weight of a rider, more weight is placed on the horse's forehand.

To make life easier for your horse, during a downward transition use a half-halt to re-engage the hindquarters, and make sure that you are sitting in balance and in a good position. If you are out of harmony with your horse it will be more difficult for him to use his quarters and he will then go down a gear with his hindlegs straggling behind him instead of coming underneath him so that he can step well into the next pace.

Horses should start working progressively through transitions, from the trot to a halt, through the walk. Acute transitions like that from a walk to a canter without an intervening trot phase, require a greater degree of balance, engagement of the quarters and impulsion.

Your schooling arena

It will be far easier to ride school movements such as turns and circles, if you have a properly marked out schooling arena. At the very least you will need to mark the four corners of your arena. If at all possible try to set aside a 60 × 120 feet (20 × 40 metre) area in your field and mark it out as a dressage arena. Sets of dressage markers are relatively inexpensive and will certainly be an aid to your schooling programme.

Unless you have a marked working area it will not be possible for you to know how accurately or otherwise you are riding circles and other movements.

For exercises such as 20 metre (60 foot) circles it is extremely helpful to mark where the line of the circle should be – with cones or boxes for example. This will ensure that your circles are of the correct shape and size.

Riding turns and circles

Turns are always parts of a circle so the same principles apply to riding them. The aids for turns and circles are basically: inside rein for direction, inside leg for impulsion and bend, outside rein for controlling the pace and bend, outside leg to control the hindquarters.

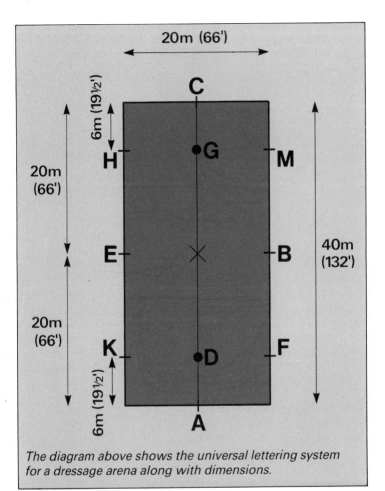

The diagram above shows the universal lettering system for a dressage arena along with dimensions.

The term 'bend' is a little misleading. We want the horse to look in the direction in which he is moving and we use the term 'bend' to describe this. However, as the horse has a rigid backbone he cannot 'bend' it. What he can do and does, providing that his training has been correct, is to contract his ribcage on the inside of the bend and then to expand it on the outside.

A common fault is for the horse to have too much 'bend' in his neck. It should be no more than in the body, i.e., the neck should be just inclined in the direction of the movement (the usual test is for the rider to just be able to see the corner of the horse's eye). The horse's hindlegs should follow in the path of the forelegs.

57

Through turns and circles, the horse should 'bend' in the direction in which he is moving.

Turns across the schooling area may be from one side to another – for example, from B to E, across the short sides, i.e., from C to A along the centre line, or across the diagonals.

Circles ridden in the schooling area may be 20, 15, 10 or 6 metres (known as voltes) in diameter or, of course, around the whole of the school or manege. It is difficult for a horse to execute a 6 metre circle properly; voltes are the province of the more experienced horse who has reached a higher level of training.

Circles of 10 metres diameter prove difficult to animals who are not sufficiently supple and balanced. Trying to do too much too soon puts strain on the horse. If your horse is falling in or out of 10 metre circles then he is not ready for this work yet and should spend more time on the basic exercises to assist his suppleness and strength.

Riding large around an arena requires that the corners of the manege be treated like sections of circles, not as distinct turns. The objective is for the horse to move through the corners without his quarters swinging out, and with the hind legs following in the tracks of the forefeet. If you try to make the corners too sharp then the horse's quarters will have to swing out.

It is quite common to see riders not using sufficient leg around a corner so the horse tends to fall in. Ride inside leg to outside hand and maintain the bend in the direction you are

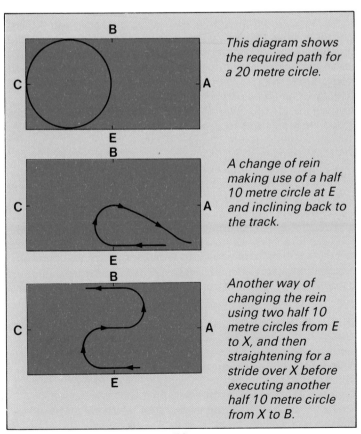

This diagram shows the required path for a 20 metre circle.

A change of rein making use of a half 10 metre circle at E and inclining back to the track.

Another way of changing the rein using two half 10 metre circles from E to X, and then straightening for a stride over X before executing another half 10 metre circle from X to B.

going. Do not try to correct the falling in by holding the horse out with the outside hand – remember that such a rein aid will encourage the horse to look to the outside, i.e. in the wrong direction.

As you ride circles and turns, even as you ride large around the arena, notice how easy it is for the horse to lose impulsion through the corners and around the circles. This is because the horse's balance has been upset by the change of direction, resulting in lost impulsion which inevitably has an effect on the rhythm of the gait in which you are working.

To counteract this you need to increase the leg aid to create more energy, but you must be careful to contain this with your hand or the extra energy will be lost. Impulsion means the harnessing and directing of the energy from the hindquarters; it does not mean an increase in the horse's speed.

Simple changes of rein, 20 metre circles, figures of eight, loops and serpentines can now be used to supple your horse. Throughout all these movements be aware of your own position. For instance, looking too far around a circle can mean that your upper body is totally out of balance with your horse. Look straight through the horse's ears and keep your shoulders and hips parallel to those of the horse. Comparatively speaking, the rider's head is a heavy object and if you are constantly looking down or to the side, you are adversely affecting your horse's balance.

When riding any circles for the first time it is well to mark them out in your arena. For a 20 metre circle from A, think of riding a diamond shape with the points of the diamond being at A, just after K, at X and just before F. Now you know which points you are aiming for – but horses cannot turn at right angles so think of rounding off each of your points.

This should help you to ride an accurate circle and the same principle can be applied to smaller circles. Once you have an accurate, properly shaped circle, you can concentrate on the horse's way of going. If your horse is falling in, his

▶ *Three loop serpentines, starting at either the C or A end of the school, involve changes of diagonal every time you pass over the centre line (A to C) if you are working in rising trot. Where the loops 'touch' the long side of the school, think of riding half 10 metre circles. To add variety, 10 metre circles can be ridden at the beginning and end of the serpentines or as additions to the loops themselves, i.e., inside each loop.*

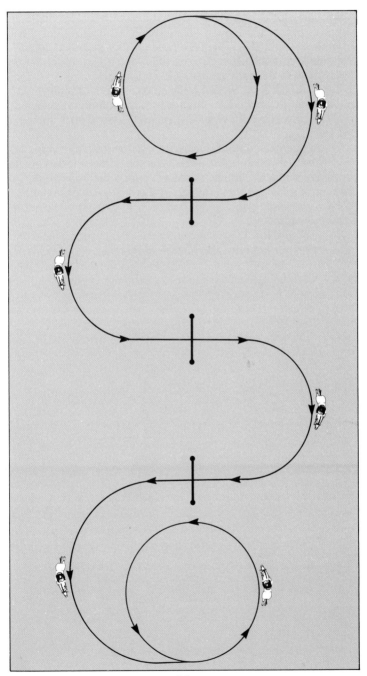

hindquarters will be carried inside the track of his forefeet. When falling out, the quarters are outside the imprint of the forefeet. Usually it is rider positional error or incorrect use of the aids that is the cause, unless the horse being ridden is very young and in the early stages of his training.

Two 20 metre circles can be used as a figure of eight, riding straight on the B–E line for a couple of metres over X so that the rider can shift weight, change the bend and change the rein.

Large circles and figures of eight may be ridden in walk, trot or canter. However, faster work magnifies rider errors. For example, when circling at a canter a rider's seat may slide outwards if his position is weak; stiff arms can restrict the horse's movement so it is difficult for him to establish a good working canter.

Once again, we have returned to the importance of the rider's position and the application of the aids.

CHAPTER FOUR

Riding out

Horses and riders alike need to take a break from serious schooling, so hacks out should be incorporated into your horse's weekly work schedule. There is more to a hack than simply being a pleasant way of giving your horse an hour and a half's exercise.

Hacking can be a pleasurable way of relaxing and letting your worries ebb away; it is a vital part of any fitness programme and it can also be an educational outing for you and your horse.

If you can, try to mix your hacks so that sometimes you ride with friends and on other occasions it is just you and your horse. Young, inexperienced horses take comfort from the presence of other horses but they should not be allowed to become totally reliant on company – they should be able to face the big world alone with their rider.

When riding a youngster in the company of others, make sure that your horse will take the lead or follow as asked – it is all good discipline for him.

Try to plan hacks into your horse's exercise programme – after all, they are the foundation work for fitness. The fitter your horse becomes, the more enjoyable your hacks out can become as you can travel further afield, exploring new areas and at faster paces.

Remember to build up your horse's fitness gradually or you could risk injuring him. If the horse has been rested he will need to be brought back into work gradually, starting off initially with walking. For instance, a horse coming back into work after a tendon injury, may need a month or more of walking before anything more strenuous is asked of him.

Take your horse's circumstances into consideration and seek the advice of your vet or a more experienced person if in any doubt, particularly if the horse has been out of action for some considerable time.

Once the walking base is established, trotting can be introduced, with the duration of the trotting sessions gradually increasing. This initial work will help to harden the horse's tendons and tone his muscles.

Another sensible precaution worth following is to walk the first and last miles. This ensures that the horse is loosened up at the start of your ride, and is brought back to his stable at the ride's completion in a dry and comfortable state.

In company some horses become very strong – use the bridging method with your reins, as shown here, so that the horse pulls against himself and not against you.

However, the exception to this is if you are riding in cold, wet weather conditions. In such circumstances, the horse may get rather cold if you walk for too long. It is therefore sensible to alternate walk and trot, keeping a careful eye on the horse's temperature. You can get a good indication of the animal's temperature by feeling his neck or ears.

Equine fitness is a book in itself – it is certainly worth learning more about the subject from the wealth of material available in books and magazines.

One point to remember: if your horse misses a few days' work, perhaps through his or your illness, or the fact that circumstances have prevented you from exercising, you must allow him time to regain his position in his fitness programme. In other words, if he has missed five days of work, do not mount him and give him a really hard exercise session. Let the horse have five days back in work and then he should be back at the point he would have reached before work ceased.

Adding interest to your hacks

Many riders find it easier to keep their horses interested and going forward when hacking than in the confines of a school. Think how much easier life could be if you schooled whilst out hacking!

Make use of features like the road side or grassy centre of a track to check whether your horse is straight. Ask him to lengthen or shorten strides between two points – telegraph poles, for instance. Insist on obedience, like standing still at road junctions. Practise your transitions. If you can find a good flat area why not work him in circles and also in figures-of-eight? All this will help your horse to become more responsive and obedient which will pay dividends when you school him in more traditional surroundings.

Improving your horse's fitness and balance

Although hacking out is intended to be enjoyable for your horse, you can take the opportunity of riding on different terrains to improve his fitness and balance.

Going up or down hills is hard work for your horse, so introduce hillwork gradually into his fitness programme. Moving uphill requires considerable power and effort from the horse: he could easily strain his hocks if allowed to rush uphill unchecked. You can assist him by inclining forward or, on very steep slopes, standing in your stirrups to take your weight off his back, using his mane or a martingale or breastplate neckstrap to aid your balance.

Keeping a horse balanced when travelling downhill is more difficult. The horse's natural tendency is to pick his way at first and then rush to complete the last few yards. You should aim at an even, steady pace throughout, by maintaining a steady contact, keeping your weight down through your legs into the stirrups, your knees and ankles acting as shock absorbers, and letting your body follow the movement of the horse.

How to ride downhill and uphill, without upsetting your horse's balance (above left). Leaning back and using the reins to balance when going downhill or refusing to take your weight off the horse's back when travelling uphill (above right) makes life more difficult for your horse.

Sit still so that you help rather than hinder your mount. Always ride either straight up or down a hill, as taking a slope on an angle could result in your horse falling.

Hazards and obstacles

Rivers, streams or fords may have to be negotiated on your rides out, particularly if you become more adventurous and opt for longer trips. Select your crossing point carefully so that you are traversing a solid stream or river bottom. If you cannot find a suitable place or are worried about the horse sinking down into the river bed it is preferable to backtrack rather than frighten and possibly injure your horse.

Boulders or slippery going on a river bed need to be crossed carefully. Fast-flowing rivers should be tackled by riding obliquely against the current.

When crossing moorlands, be on the look-out for patches of boggy ground, often conspicuous as they are a brighter colour than the surrounding fern and heather. Wet layers of moss or soil over rocks can also make for slippery going.

Gates

Riding out inevitably means dealing with gates, and these can be a most frustrating obstacle. Gates that are hanging off their hinges or are tied up with more string and knots than you knew existed are impossible to tackle from horseback. It is much easier to dismount and cope with the hazard.

However, it is quite simple to deal with normal gates while remaining mounted, once you know the correct way. Position your horse with his head facing the latch so that you can bend down easily to undo the gate. Keep your reins short, taking them and your whip in one hand, while you undo the latch with the other hand.

Now, using your leg nearest the gate, push your horse away from the gate so that he executes a turn on the forehand. Open the gate so that you can pass through easily, bearing in mind that some horses tend to rush through, and you do not want to risk being pushed or pulled off.

Once through, position your horse parallel to the gate again, as before, so that you can pull the gate to and refasten the latch. A point to be careful of throughout this procedure is

Training your horse to behave at gates makes hacking out much more enjoyable.

the position of your horse's head: it is very easy for a martingale or rein to get caught over the latch which could result in an upset horse and a nasty accident.

Other hazards

Bridleways may pass through fields of livestock, so care must be taken here. Ride quietly and slowly and the chances are that the animals will not bother with you. Frisky bullocks,

68

Take advantage of natural features like streams, but always check the take-off and landing sides of fences.

however, can present a problem, particularly if your horse has not seen them before. Try to introduce the horse to cattle by riding through with friends on more cow-proof animals, or let the horse meet the animals over the fence first.

If cattle or sheep gather round a gate that you have to open, it is easier to dismount to open the gate. This also gives you the chance to 'shoo' the animals out of the way to eliminate

Always ride your horse forwards properly as otherwise he may catch you out if he spooks at a barking dog or other similar hazard, especially in traffic.

any chance of them slipping through the gate as you open it.

Ditches or fallen logs may present inviting jumps, but always check the landing and take-off sides before jumping. Never jump on to private land, and avoid anything too ambitious if you are riding out alone. If you do have an accident, you really are in trouble! As a precautionary measure, some riders do attach identity discs to their horse's saddle and bridle so that if they fall and the horse runs loose, any person catching the horse would see the address and telephone number, or know which stable yard to contact.

Riding through villages often means encountering barking dogs, noisy lawnmowers, playing children and other 'ghosts' such as flapping laundry, plastic bags and so on. Usually you can feel if your horse is going to 'spook': his head rises, the steps become shorter and he starts 'looking' or 'peeping' well in advance of the offending object. Do not hesitate, but ride your horse forward positively. Keep your legs on, look straight

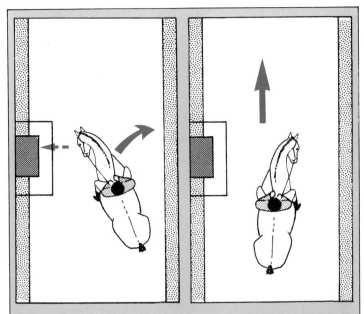

If your horse turns to look at a 'ghost or spook' object and then shies, he will shy into traffic (above left). If you look ahead and keep your horse's head turned away from a potential 'spook' then the direction of movement will be forwards (above right).

ahead, and use your whip and voice if necessary to encourage the horse forward.

Be prepared

Whenever and wherever you are riding, it is as well to be prepared. Always carry a hoofpick, a piece of baler twine (for emergency repairs should your bridle break) and coins for the telephone in an emergency.

Hacks out can, of course, be varied by turning them into picnic or pub rides – numnahs with pockets or specially designed saddle bags can be bought. These are certainly worth investing in so that you can carry maps, waterproofs and food easily.

Riding on the roads in winter presents the added hazards of poor visibility, snow and ice. Naturally you will try to avoid

71

riding out at dusk or when it is dark but such an occasion could arise if you have been delayed on a hack, or when you are riding in conditions of poor visibility.

Be prepared for this by always carrying in your pocket some of the fluorescent tabs that can be fitted on to your horse's

Be prepared for riding in failing light – fluorescent gear is easily carried in your pocket.

legs and tail, or on to your arms and hat. Safety gear is very reasonably priced, light and easy to carry.

For the autumn and winter you may like to invest in some of the brushing boots now available which also have fluorescent strips on them. These boots have the dual purpose of giving your horse leg protection as well as ensuring good visibility.

However, the best safety measure of all is to avoid riding on the roads after dark or in poor weather conditions. If you have to ride on icy roads, fit knee boots on to your horse for extra protection in case he does fall. Ensure that the top strap is securely fitted while the lower strap should allow for movement of the knee. Fitted correctly, knee boots should not slip down and cause a hazard.

Riding in snow presents the problem of snow balling in the horse's hooves so that the horse ends up tottering along on snowy stilts. Packing grease into the animal's hooves before you set off for a ride helps a little.

Even in decent weather conditions, the surface of some roads is not ideal for horses. Tarmac may have become so

Roads can be slippery but usually the edges offer a reasonable amount of grip.

smooth that it is safest to stay in walk. Usually the edge of the road offers more grip, because it is rougher. If you are on a really steep slippery road it is as well to dismount and lead your horse.

Grass verges can hide hazards such as broken glass or small drainage ditches so beware of cantering along on verges. It is all too easy to injure your horse.

Consult your farrier about fitting road studs. These are small studs that provide extra grip as they have tungsten carbide tipped ends. Normally one or two studs are fitted in each hind shoe of the horse.

Riding in traffic

Horses playing up on roads are dangerous. Some 'spooky' horses are just teasing their riders and need firm correction to get them out of the habit; others, particularly if they are youngsters, are genuinely wary or even frightened and need careful handling to educate them about the big world.

Spooky horses like to have a good look at everything but they can be unpredictable, sometimes playing up at the slightest excuse, like a leaf bowling along the road due to the wind, whilst on other occasions allowing something like a tractor to go by without even appearing to notice it.

You need to accustom your spooky animal to all kinds of sights and sounds. If you can, arrange for him to graze in a paddock that adjoins a busy road so he gets used to buses, lorries and motorcycles screeching past. This is also a useful lesson for young horses – it is a much safer way of introducing them to heavier traffic than venturing straight out on to the roads.

When you hack out and your horse spooks you can either let him stop and inspect the 'problem' item or ride him forwards strongly, using your legs and voice positively, backed up by your whip if necessary.

The problem with spooky horses is that they can be very dangerous if they play up on busy roads. It is quite possible that the horse's back end may swing into the path of traffic; to avoid this, keep the horse's head away from the object of which he is afraid. If his head is turned towards the road then his back end will stay towards the verge.

Young or green horses often act up through a lack of confidence. The big world can be quite a frightening place, with children leaping out at them to say hello, strange signs

Learn your Highway Code before venturing out on the roads. When turning right riders must stay on the left-hand side of the road, rather than moving into the middle as you would if in a car or on a bicycle.

on the roadside, traffic passing by, barking dogs, and other distractions.

Do not try to traffic-proof a youngster without the help of other more experienced riders and horses. By riding out in a group, the young horse can be placed in the middle where he will feel more secure. He should be introduced gradually to roadwork, starting with quiet roads, where he will be able to follow the example of the older, more experienced horses.

All riders should avoid busy main roads if it is at all possible – no matter how traffic-proof your horse, accidents can and do happen.

Where to ride in Britain

This can pose a problem. Inevitably some road work will be required, so you must know how to behave on the highway. The British Horse Society runs Riding & Road Safety tests,

usually organized by the local county branch or a riding club. These normally involve an instructional evening with a film show and possibly some practice sessions before the actual test is taken. The Society also publishes a booklet on the subject (see Bibliography).

The quality of off-road riding varies considerably according to where you live. Local bridleways can be found using the Pathfinder maps from the Ordnance Survey 1:25,000 series. You may find that although the bridleways are marked on the map, actual signs on the ground are not so evident.

Throughout Britain local bridleways associations are trying to ensure that local rights of way are kept open, in good repair and are well marked. Contacting your local representative, or the County Bridleways Officer of the British Horse Society, is

When the going is good, riding on bridleways gives your horse the chance to enjoy breezing along.

a good step in establishing routes for you to ride along and enjoy. In England and Wales public rights of way are divided into: public footpaths, which are for walkers only; bridleways, on which you may go on foot, horseback or pedal cycle; byways (usually old roads) and public roads, on which all traffic is permitted.

Near older towns and cities, where there are commons it is sometimes possible to ride on these, but check with your Local Authority. It is also possible to use, by local or established custom or consent, areas of open country like moorland, beaches, some woods and forests and country parks – again, check with the local council. The Countryside Commission produces a useful booklet, giving advice on where you can go and what you can do (see Bibliography).

The British Horse Society also has an Access and Rights of Way division which offers help and advice linked to the Society's network of County Bridleways Officers. In addition, numerous bridleways groups and associations are to be found all over the United Kingdom.

If you have a country park or Forestry Commission land nearby, ask if riders are allowed. A permit may be required; in some cases these are free, in others a small charge is made.

Check with the relevant local authority to see if beach riding is allowed as it provides a superb day out for you and your horse.

Farmers are becoming increasingly aware of the advantages of opening up their land to riders. A number of purpose-made and set-aside licensed tracks have become available – ask your local riding club or bridleways group for any local amenities.

Some farmers are quite willing to allow horse riders access to their land. If you could connect a bridleways route by riding across some private land then speak to the landowner. He may ask for a small annual payment but if it provides a good ride and keeps you off the busy roads, surely it is worth considering?

Another organization that is providing safe off-road riding, with the added attraction of well-built, optional jumps, is UK Chasers, which organizes courses around the country.

An anual fee is paid to UK Chasers and a daily fee to the landowner. These courses are ideal for simply hacking or for schooling your horse over well-built fences (for more information, see the Useful Addresses section at the back of the book).

The Country Code

- Enjoy the countryside and respect its life and work.
- Guard against all risk of fire.
- Fasten all gates.
- Keep your dogs under close control.
- Keep to public paths across farmland.
- Use gates and stiles to cross fences, hedges and walls.
- Leave livestock, crops and machinery alone.
- Take your litter home.
- Help to keep all water clean.
- Protect wildlife, plants and trees.
- Take special care on country roads.
- Make no unnecessary noise.

Bibliography

Books

British Horse Society: *Riding Safely on the Roads*
Countryside Commission: *Out in the Country*
Eccles, Lesley: *A Guide to Horse Riding*
(Patrick Stephens 1988)
Harris, Charles: *Fundamentals of Riding*
(J. A. Allen & Co 1985)
Rees, Lucy: *The Horse's Mind* (Stanley Paul)
Thelwall, Jane: *The Less-than-Perfect Horse* (Methuen 1987)

Magazines and publications

Horse & Pony Magazine (EMAP Pursuit Publishing Ltd,
Bretton Court, Bretton, Peterborough, PE2 0XW
Horse World & Rider (Brisbane, Queensland, Australia).
Your Horse Magazine (EMAP Pursuit Publishing Ltd,
Bretton Court, Bretton, Peterborough, PE2 0XW

Useful addresses

**Association of
British Riding Schools**
Old Brewery Yard
Penzance
Cornwall TR18 2SL

British Horse Society
The British Equestrian Centre
Stoneleigh
Kenilworth
Warwickshire
CV8 2LR

Countryside Commission
Publications Despatch
Department
19-23 Albert Road
Manchester M19 2EQ

UK Chasers
Lower Farm
Otmoor Lane
Beckley
Oxon OX3 9TD